Volume 5
Decodable
Reader

Mc
Graw
Hill
Education

Bothell, WA • Chicago, IL • Columbus, OH • New York, NY

Contents

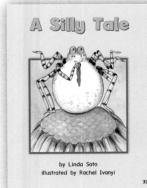

Ray and Gail Help

retold by Susan Martina

illustrated by Brenda Johnson

One day Ray went out to play. He came to a lake.

"I will stop to get a drink," he said. "Then I'll be on my way."

2

Ray got off the trail. Splash!
He fell in.

"Help!" yelled Ray. "I can not
swim well."

Just then Gail came by.

"I will help!" she yelled back.

Gail gave Ray a blade of grass.
Ray got on. He went up, up, up!

Ray was wet but safe.

"Thanks!" said Ray. "I must be on my way."

"I wish you could stay," said Gail.

But just then Ray saw a big
cat. It was waving its tail.
That cat wanted to eat Gail!

Ray used his brain. He bit that big cat on its leg.

The cat yelled in pain! Ray saved Gail.

"That was close!" said Gail. "Can you stay and play?"

"Yes I can," said Ray.

Then Ray and Gail played. They stayed friends until this day.

8

Friday Night Fun

by Michelle Evans

illustrated by Barbara J. Counseller

It was Friday night! A bright
white moon sat up high in the
sky. My pals and I ran with all
our might. Friday night is time
for fun!

"Look at those rides! Let's try
and ride them all!" Ty yelled.

"I like the kind of ride that
sends me up high. Let's take
the highest ride!" I cried.

"Let's fly on this ride!" yelled Tom.

We got tickets and went high.

"Let's try to find Mom," I said
when we finished. "Hi, Mom!"

It is late. Mom tells us it is time to go home. My pals and I liked the lights. We liked the big rides.

The next night we went out again!

"I have a plan," said Mom.

"Will we see bright lights?" I asked.

"Yes!" Mom said.

14

"Do you like these bright lights
in Mike's ice cream shop?"
Mom asked.

"Yes!" we exclaim. "Mike's is the
best place!"

15

Then what did I spy? A big cat named Linus came by. A night with rides is fun. But a night with ice cream, pals, and Linus is the nicest kind of night.

A Boat That Floats

by Anthony Collins

illustrated by Jan Pyk

Joan lived on Cold Cove. The homes sat in a row on Doe Road. Joan's cat, Joe, napped while boats floated past.

One day, Joan strolled to the dock.

"It is Boat Show Day!" Mr. Poe said.

"We will show the most boats on the coast!" Mrs. Poe added.

"I own this rowboat," said Mrs. Poe.

"Can I get in?" asked Joan.

"We will both go in," said Mrs. Poe.
"I'll row."

She rowed and rowed. Then a
patched-up hole broke open. Water
flowed in the boat.

"No!" groaned Mrs. Poe.

"The boat is getting low. Let's make the load less!" yelled Mrs. Poe. "Let's throw out this rope!"

Mrs. Poe and Joan waved at
a boat.

"It's Mr. Poe!" yelled Joan. "Help
us. This boat will not float!"

Mr. Poe picked them up.

"I will own a boat one day,"
said Joan.

"What kind?" asked Mr. Poe.

Joan smiled. "A boat that floats!"

A Clean Beach

by Cassandra Barrett

illustrated by Barbara Counseller

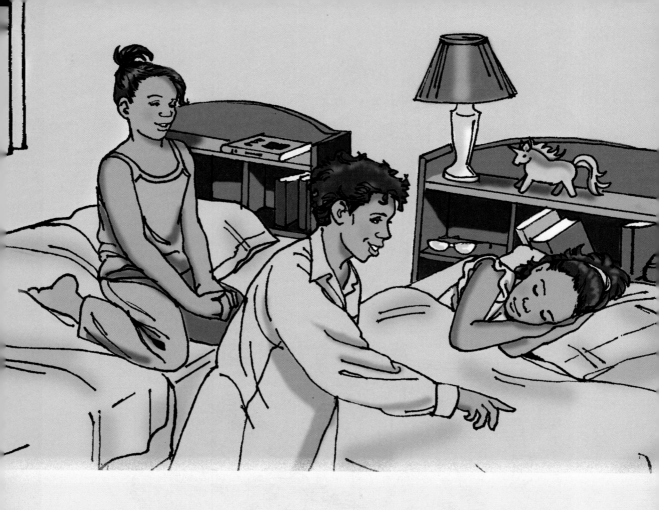

Mom woke us up. "Get up, Dee! Get up, Jean!"

"But it isn't time," we said.

"No sleeping in today. We are going to the beach!" said Mom.

We sat in the back seat.
Mom told us to dress in jeans.

"Why?" I asked.

"You will see," said Mom.

When we got to the beach,
I ran to the sand. I could
smell the sea. I could feel the
breeze. Then Mom showed us
why we had come.

A man held a sign. It said, "Clean up your beach. Please help!"

"We need to clean up," Jean said.

I agreed.

The man asked us to please put
the trash in the bags. He told
us to leave shells, rocks, and
seaweed on the beach.

We picked up bags, cans, and junk.
Mom picked up a green bottle.
We filled three bags with trash.
Then we piled the bags in a heap.

We had a seat on the beach
and rested.

Mom said, "Wasn't that fun?
Now the beach is clean! I
hope it will stay that way."

A Silly Tale

by Linda Soto

illustrated by Rachel Ivanyi

Spiders we see today have tiny waists. But that was not always the way. This tale tells us how spiders got such tiny waists.

It was a sunny day. Granddaddy
Spider studied the bees. The
bees were getting sticky, golden
dust from a daisy.

"What will you do with that sticky dust?" asked Granddaddy.

"It's for a feast," the bees buzzed.

"What feast?" Granddaddy asked.

He quickly called his grand kids.

The spider babies asked, "Why did you ask for us Granddaddy?"

"Who is hosting a feast?" asked Granddaddy.

"It is Donkey," said a tiny spider.

"It is Elephant," said the next.

"It is Chimp," said the next.

"It is Zebra," said the last.

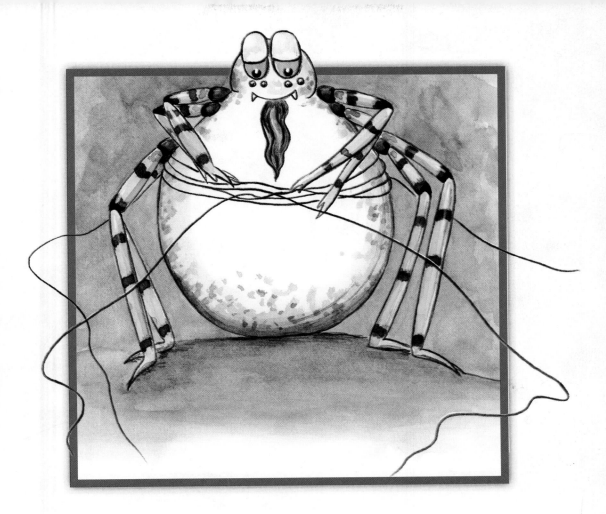

Granddaddy had a plan. He spun
four silky lines. He tied each line
around his tummy. He gave each
spider baby a line.

"When a feast begins, give a tug.
Then I will know where it is."

Four feasts began at the same time.
The tiny babies tugged. The lines
squeezed Granddaddy. Then the
lines snapped! Granddaddy's waist
was tiny. And it remains tiny to
this day!

A Few Shops on
Mule Lane

by Maurice Jenkins

illustrated by Mary Kurnick Maass

The sun is shining. It is a bright
June day. Music wakes me up.
I know what we'll be doing today.

Dad is singing a song.

"Hi, cutie!" he sings. He flips a few pancakes. "Did my music wake you?"

"I'm going to Mule Lane, Ivy." said Dad. "Would you like to come with me?"

"Yes," I smiled. "I'll eat a few more pancakes. I'll need the fuel."

The sun shines high in the sky.
It gives Mule Lane a yellow hue.
I hear a song from the music shop.
I see a bake shop. It is a fine day
on Mule Lane.

We get the mail. Dad lets me
use the key. I open the mailbox.
I see a few letters inside and
take them.

We look inside the bake shop!

I ask, "Dad, can we go in?"

"Yes, we can," Dad replies.

We leave with a huge sandwich and a few treats!

We end up at the Value Shop.
Dad helps me find a cute costume.
I will use it for my show at school.
We had a fun day on Mule Lane.

Volume 5

Decodable Words

Target Phonics Elements: Long *a: ai, ay*

brain, day, Gail, pain, play, played, Ray, stay, tail, trail, way

High-Frequency Words

Review: *be, by, could, eat, he, one, out, said, the, they, to, wanted, was, you*

Story Words

friends, saw

Decodable Words

Target Phonics Element: Long *i: i, igh, ie, y*

bright, cried, fly, Friday, hi, high, highest, kind, light, Linus, might, my, night, sky, try, Ty

High-Frequency Words

Review: *again, be, do, go, look, me, of, or, our, out, said, the, to, see, we, you*

Story Words

cream

Decodable Words

Target Phonics Elements: Long *o: o, ow, oa, oe*
boats, both, coast, cold, Doe, floated, flowed, go, groan, load, low, most, no, open, own, Poe, row, rowboat, show, stroll, told, throw

High-Frequency Words

Review: *one, out, said, to, water, we, what, you*

Decodable Words

Target Phonics Elements: Long *e: e_e, ee, ea, e*
agreed, beach, breeze, clean, Dee, feel, green, he, heap, Jean, jeans, leave, need, please, sea, seaweed, seat, see, sleeping, the, three, we

High-Frequency Words

Review: *are, come, could, now, said, put, today, to, was, you, your*

Story Words

bottle, sneakers

Decodable Words

Target Phonics Elements: Long e: *y, ey*
baby, daisy, Donkey, Grandaddy, silky, sticky, sunny, tiny, tummy

High-Frequency Words

Review: *always, around, called, for, four, from, have, know, said, their, to, today, was, were, what, where, who, you*

Story Words
elephant, spider

Decodable Words

Target Phonics Elements: Long u: *u_e, ew, u, ue*
cute, cutie, fuel, few, hue, huge, June, Mule, music, use, Value

High-Frequency Words

Review: *come, doing, from, now, look, more, now, said, today, too, what, would, you*

Story Words
hear, school, letters

Decoding skills taught to date:

Phonics: Short *a*; Short *i*; Short *o*; Short *e*, Short *u*;
l- Blends; *r-* Blends; *s* -Blends; End Blends; Long *a*: *a_e;*
Long *i*: *i_e*; Long *o*: *o_e*; Long *u*: *u_e;* Soft *c*, Soft *g ,-dge*;
Consonant Digraphs: *th, sh, -ng*; Consonant Digraphs:
ch, -tch, wh, ph; Three-Letter Blends; Long *a*: *ai, ay*; Long
i: *i, igh, ie, y*; Long *o*: *o, ow, oa, oe*; Long *e*: *e_e, ee, ea, e, ie*;
Long *e*: *y, ey*; Long *u*: *u_e, ew, u, ue*

Structural Analysis: Plural Nouns *-s;* Inflectional
Ending *-s;* Plural Nouns *-es;* Inflectional Ending *-es;* Closed
Syllables; Inflectional Ending *-ed* ; Inflectional Ending
-ing; Possessives (singular); Inflectional Endings *-ed, -ing*
(drop finale *e*); Inflectional Endings *-ed, -ing* (double final
consonant); CVCe syllables; Prefixes *re-, un-, dis-*; Suffixes
-ful, -less; Compound Words; Contractions with *'s, 're, 'll,
've*; Open Syllables; Contractions with *not (isn't, aren't,
wasn't, weren't, hasn't, haven't, can't)*; Inflectional Endings
and Plurals (change *y* to *i*); Comparative Inflectional
Endings *-er, -est*